Manhood Mangood

A Healing Conversation

Warren Watkins, Jr.

MANHOOD

A Healing Conversation

MANGOOD

WARREN WATKINS, JR.

Manhood Mangood
by Warren Watkins, Jr.

Cover design by Senir Design. Contact info: info@senirdesign.com.

CLF Publishing Collaborative, LLC
Hesperia, CA 92345
Visit us at clfpublishing.org

First Edition: May 2026
ISBN 979-8-9925784-5-4 (paperback)

Let The Ink Fall - (In honor of my dad)

As it was said back in the day: "The apple doesn't fall far from the tree." But in this case, the ink doesn't drip far from the pen. What am I talking about? Listen closely, it would be some thirty-nine years after the death of my parents that while at a family gathering, I found out about my dad's awesome skills. He wasn't just a good mechanic. He was also an extraordinary artist who drew all sorts of pictures. Ninny, one of my sisters, inherited that skill. I, on the other hand, inherited a separate set of artistic skills: literary arts, martial arts, and recording arts. My youngest son Rico inherited some of each art: literary arts, martial arts, and visual arts (drawing, painting, sketching, etc). He would go on to be recognized in the National Junior Honor Arts Society.

Special Dedication

This book is dedicated to you, man, the reader!
A special dedication also goes out to all the
men who have had a positive
influence in my life, both living and departed.
I may not be able to name all of you,
but you and I know the role you've played in
my story. For that, I thank you, sir.
Robert R. Watkins, Edgar Smith Sr., Warren
Watkins, Sr., Courtlandt A. Deskins (Mr. C.),
Jesse F. Watkins, Lewis Johnson, Sidney
Johnson, Kenneth C. Parker, Willie "Bam"
Johnson, Leroy Taylor, Garcia Davis, and
Jerome Dyson Wright.
May God continue to bless you all.
It is my hope and prayer that, through this
book,
I have represented you well.

Forever grateful,
Warren Watkins, Jr

CONTENTS

From the Author 9

Introduction 11

Chapter 1 15
A Healing Conversation

Chapter 2 23
Intellectual Wisdom

Chapter 3 31
Go For It, Man

Chapter 4 39
Don't Be a Bitter; Be a Better Man

Chapter 5 45
Act Right

Chapter 6 51
The Post and The Most

Chapter 7 57
Manhood 101

About the Author 63

From the Author

I once heard it said, "Men speak words, but women experience them - words, that is!" So, if I were you, my brother, I'd be very careful about what you say to her and how you say it (IJS - I'm just saying). Choose your words wisely.

So, enjoy your reading, my brother, and even my sister who may read this for her own purposes. Enjoy, enjoy, and I humbly thank you in advance.

I can only speak or write about what I know and/or have experienced in my lifetime. At the time of this writing, I've had 53-plus years on this earth. So, as I began to write what we all know as stories through rap songs, for me, they grew into stories, poems, and eventually books. Lucky for me, I've always loved to read, but it was even more enjoyable creating them, from piecing together an idea, to coming up with the title, to structuring the stories from beginning, middle, and end with a little wordplay here and there. Even to this day, I still write everything longhand at first, pen and paper (usually on a legal pad). I like the freedom and space it gives me to create, sometimes even "vomiting" onto the page. Because becoming an author back in my younger days was a big deal.

During the writing of this book, I was in a prophetic space, between hurt and humility with God, where He allowed me to write down how I was feeling and what I was experiencing. Then, He said, "Go back and insert My word." And that's exactly what I did. Although I'm not a biblical scholar of any kind, I did some research, some may agree and others may not. But with the guidance of the Lord, here it is. I present to you *Manhood Mangood*.

Introduction

I engage in conversation with my brothers, men of all colors. We communicate in a language that only we truly understand. Even if it's just for a few moments, something meaningful happens in that time. We gain understanding. We break barriers. We push ourselves to climb higher among our peers. These exchanges are often unplanned, yet deeply impactful, moments where honesty replaces pretense and real life is spoken without filters. There is a shared rhythm in these conversations, a mutual respect that allows us to speak freely about our struggles, our victories, and the lessons we are still learning along the way.

Through these conversations, we continue to research and learn more about life, about what it is, and what it means to grow into manhood. These are not surface-level discussions; they are reflections shaped by experience, accountability, and the desire to become better men. We challenge one another. We sharpen one another. We hold up mirrors that reveal both strengths and areas in need of growth. In doing so, we begin to understand that manhood is not defined by age alone, but by responsibility, discipline, character, and purpose.

This is the foundation of *Manhood Mangood*. It is built on real conversations, real perspectives, and real transformation. It is about confronting the truths that are often avoided and addressing the standards that must be established if we are to grow into men of substance. These dialogues create a space where growth is not only encouraged, but expected, a space where excuses are dismantled and accountability is embraced.

One man, D.J., once said, "I don't date broke women because they don't bring anything to the table, but they expect everything." While his statement may seem direct, it opens the door to a broader conversation about expectations, contributions, and personal responsibility. It forces us to examine not only what we desire in others, but what we ourselves are bringing to the table. These are the kinds of statements that spark deeper dialogue, pushing us to evaluate our standards, our mindset, and our approach to relationships.

In this space, nothing is off limits. We talk about life, relationships, finances, purpose, and identity. We wrestle with hard truths and celebrate hard-earned growth. And through it all, we are reminded that manhood is a journey, one that is best navigated not in isolation, but in brotherhood.

Chapter 1

A Healing Conversation

Chapter 1
A Healing Conversation

Manhood Mangood is a deep and honest conversation, one that challenges men to reflect on what it truly means to be in control of themselves, their emotions, and their lives. It's about understanding what makes a man feel like a man, not just on the surface, but at his core. This is not a casual exchange of ideas; it is a call to self-examination, accountability, and growth. It invites men to look inward, confront what has been ignored, and begin the process of becoming intentional about who they are becoming.

This conversation touches on how a man presents himself, through his dress, his work ethic, his speech, his language, and his interactions with others, especially women. Growth in these areas doesn't happen overnight, but it does happen with intention and effort. There is wisdom to be gained from lived experiences and from the words of others, including works like *Introducing The Secret Pen* by Warren Watkins, Jr., *Don't Give Up On You, Thug Blvd.,* and *Emotional Man*. These voices, along with personal reflection, help shape a more complete understanding of identity, responsibility, and maturity.

Let's begin with something many men were never taught: It's okay to hurt. And it's okay to cry. In Book of Psalms 3:4–5, it says: *"I cried out to the Lord with my voice, and He heard me from His holy hill. Selah. I lay down and slept; I awoke, for the Lord sustained me."* That doesn't make you weak; it makes you human. At the end of the day, you're still a man. The difference is that now, you're an empowered man, one who understands his emotions instead of hiding from them. And through that growth, you become capable of helping another brother navigate his own struggles. Emotional awareness does not diminish masculinity; it refines it.

Now, let's address something important: Why do some women hesitate to speak or engage? Often, it's because of past experiences of being approached the wrong way, too often, or without respect. Here's a simple but powerful shift: Try speaking with sincerity and respect. Use polite language. Approach with intention, not pressure. You may be surprised at how differently you're received. Respect opens doors that force will never unlock. For more helpful hints, refer to *Introducing The Secret Pen*. Communication is not just about expression. It is about impact, tone, and awareness of how your presence affects others.

On the other hand, let's talk about preparation, especially when it comes to work and opportunity. Preparation reflects one's mindset before it is ever a reflection of appearance. Here are a few pointers:

- Pull up your pants and present yourself with pride.
- Keep yourself well-groomed.
- Dress with purpose, whether that's a suit or clean, appropriate casual wear.
- Be ready to communicate your skills and value clearly.

Remember, when you're applying for a job, you're asking someone to trust you to represent their company. That matters. Presentation speaks before words do. It communicates discipline, awareness, and self-respect. I tell my sons and daughters the same thing: Your attitude plays a major role in your success. Your mindset often determines whether opportunity recognizes you or passes you by.

I remember when I didn't have a job, the long process, the waiting, the uncertainty. But I also learned this: If you care enough to get the job, you should care enough to show up on time and give your best once you have it. Consistency after opportunity is just as important as effort before it.

To every man reading this: Try these principles. Apply them. Then, step back and observe what changes. Ask yourself honestly: Do I deserve this? Or do I deserve better? Only you and God truly know your situation and maybe a few people you trust. But as it says in Epistle of James 2:17, "Faith, if it hath not works, is dead, being alone." So ask yourself: How much work are you willing to put in? Transformation requires action, not just awareness.

Blake B. once said: "Women often give love freely. Men give respect, but their love must be earned." Whether one agrees fully or not, it raises an important reflection on how love, respect, and accountability function in relationships. These are not automatic. They are cultivated through behavior, consistency, and character.

Take a moment and sit with your thoughts. Ask yourself one of the most important questions you'll ever face: Why am I here? Your answer should lead you to this truth: You are the CEO of your life. You can't control everything, but you can control yourself. And that's where it begins, with self-governance, discipline, and ownership.

Let's be real:

- You want nice clothes, right?
- You want a reliable, maybe even stylish car, right?
- You want a lavish home?
- You want financial stability?

None of that comes without effort. No one is going to hand it to you. This is where focus comes in. Every day, you make a choice between negative and positive energy. And those choices shape your outcomes, from how you carry yourself to the decisions you make. The results? They're on you. So take ownership. Stay focused. Put in the work.

Good luck, and stay committed to becoming your best self.

CHAPTER 2

INTELLECTUAL WISDOM
(YOUNG MINDS)

CHAPTER 2
INTELLECTUAL WISDOM (YOUNG MINDS)

I'm speaking to you from many angles - about us, to us, and for us. Who knows who this may help? So no, I won't stop talking to us about us. It's both my mission and my pleasure. This dialogue is not limited to a single perspective or experience; it is layered, lived, and reflective of many voices, many journeys, and many lessons learned along the way.

As a man, you will encounter pain at some point in your life. That's not a possibility; it's a guarantee. The question is not if, but how you will respond. You must take that pain and use it to rise above the odds. Turn something negative into something meaningful. No matter how long it takes, you keep going. Because whether it's spoken or unspoken, that's what is expected of you as a man. Pain becomes a proving ground, not a place of permanent residence. It shapes you, but it should not break you. It refines your character, your patience, and your ability to endure.

Let me give you a few real-life examples to think about.

Tyrese once said, "I almost lost my daughter in twenty minutes because of jealous family members. All because I have good credit, a new car, and a good job." All I could say to him in that moment was, "God's got you. You're going to be alright." Especially when you know you've done nothing wrong. Still, for the sake of clearing your name, you go through the process. You endure the investigation. And in the end, the truth rises to the top. There is something powerful about standing in truth when everything around you feels uncertain.

A few days later, that is exactly what happened. He was proven innocent. He had done nothing wrong. That was more than just a personal victory; that was a win for hard-working fathers everywhere, men of all ages, backgrounds, and walks of life, across the world. It spoke to the quiet battles many men fight, battles that are often unseen, misunderstood, or misrepresented.

Not long after that, I spoke with a young man, who was seventeen years old. For the sake of this story, we'll call him "Man-Man." I asked him a few questions. First, I asked: "If you had the opportunity to say something positive to the young men in your circle or your age group, what would you say?" He responded, "The same thing doesn't work for everybody. You have to speak to what people are actually going through." That answer alone revealed a level of awareness many overlook. Then I asked: "How does it feel to be a young father?" He paused and said, "I think I should've waited. But, I can't take it back now." That moment carried both honesty and weight, the reality of decisions that cannot be reversed, only managed. Finally, I asked: "How will you handle your situation?"

He looked me in the eye and said, "I have to grow up fast and be a good example for my son. I'm going to handle this with everything I've got and do my best to give him everything he needs." My response was simple: "Thank you." Because in that moment, you just heard the reality that many young men between the ages of 17 and 30 face every single day. And trust me there's more where that came from. There is a shared story unfolding across generations of responsibility arriving early, pressure shaping identity, and growth being demanded before preparation feels complete.

Now, let me take you back for a moment. While I was living in California, I had a best friend named John. May he rest in peace. He was married to a woman who was a well-known celebrity; however, I won't mention her name.

John would often talk to me about her, about how much he loved her, how good she was to him, even from a distance. Her work caused her to travel constantly, but they stayed connected. Sometimes, she would call while I was around, and over time, I became like extended family. There was a bond formed not just through friendship, but through trust, consistency, and shared respect.

Years passed, five, to be exact. Then, life called me back home to Baltimore because of a family emergency, and I had to leave California. One day, while I was back home, I received a long-distance call. On the other end was John's wife. She told me that John had passed away from a stroke. I was in shock. Grief has a way of freezing time in a moment you are never prepared for.

When I left California, he was full of life, healthy, motivated, and doing well. His business was thriving, and he was even working on a book. He was the kind of friend who would drop everything to take me to or from the airport without hesitation. That's the kind of man he was. Dependable. Present. Loyal.

Here's what stayed with me the most: I never met his wife face-to-face. Not once. But love connected all of us in the end. We were brought together by what we shared: a deep respect and love for John. My love for him was brotherly, platonic. Hers was deeper in a different way, physical, emotional, and rooted in marriage. Yet, both were real. Both mattered. Different expressions of love, but still anchored in one life that impacted us both.

Interestingly, they lived in separate cities within the same state. That takes trust. That takes faith. That takes a man secure in who he is, grounded in his beliefs, and confident in his relationship with both God and his wife. That's powerful love. It reflects a level of maturity and stability that many strive for but few truly maintain.

After his passing, she reached out to me. In that moment, we became connected in a new way. We were two people honoring the life of someone we both cared about deeply. We spoke about his impact: in business, in friendship, and in life. Our conversation became a space of remembrance, healing, and shared gratitude for the time we had known him.

He didn't talk much about everything, but he often spoke about his mother, who had passed shortly before I met him. That kind of loss shapes a man. And yet, he still chose to live with love, generosity, and purpose. That's what love does. That's what a good man looks like. It does not erase pain, but it teaches you how to carry it with dignity.

John, may you rest in peace, my brother.

Chapter 3

Go For It, Man

CHAPTER 3
GO FOR IT, MAN

If you're reading this and really listening, putting yourself in someone else's shoes, you can begin to understand how real men carry themselves. Whether good or bad, we all have flaws. Yes, even you, Mr. High and Mighty. You're not the only one. This is not written to condemn, but to confront with honesty, because growth begins where denial ends. When a man is willing to see himself clearly, without excuses or distortion, that is where transformation can begin.

Even after falling down and getting back up, you can still do something great. Because you are somebody. Somebody with skills, talent, and truly awesome capabilities. You just have to reach deep down inside and pull them out; that's all. I dare you to try it. You might surprise yourself with what you're capable of creating and with how the world responds to it. Too many men underestimate what is already inside of them, waiting to be developed, disciplined, and directed. Potential without action remains unrealized, but potential activated becomes purpose.

To be honest, keeping it real, there's nothing worse than a lazy man, for any reason. A man who doesn't want anything ends up with nothing. And if he isn't trying to do anything to get something, then he stays stuck. Maybe this is you. And maybe you have a child or children watching you. That alone should cause reflection, not shame, but awareness. Because stagnation does not only affect the man; it affects everyone connected to him. Responsibility is not just about provision; it is about example.

A man's life is always teaching something, whether he intends it or not. His habits, his effort, his discipline, and his direction all become lessons to those who observe him closely. The question then becomes: what are you teaching? Are you modeling growth, persistence, and accountability, or resignation, delay, and avoidance?

There is still time to shift. There is still room to rise. But it requires honesty first. It requires the courage to admit where things are, and the willingness to do something different moving forward. Because greatness is not reserved for a select few; it is built by those who decide to act.

Let me share with you a very important poem.

A Great Dad

Let it be said. As a young man
I fathered many.
Four of which were my own whereas
others hadn't any.
I did it from my heart.
So, there are no regrets.
Whether good or bad.
Let it be said that I was "A Great Dad."

I once had the opportunity to pray with a brother after a conversation we shared. Unbeknownst to me at the time, while I was praying for him, I was also being blessed internally by God. The very prayer I offered for someone else came back and strengthened me. In that sacred exchange, I was reminded that ministry is never one-directional; what you pour out in obedience often returns as personal renewal, encouragement, and spiritual reinforcement.

I'm often blessed to talk with brothers, both young and old, as they pass by my job site, you know, the one that pays the bills at home. And in those moments, we sometimes talk about how important it is to conduct yourself properly in the workplace and in life. It requires you to keep your behavior in order and your character intact. Because sooner or later, the powers that be will test you. Not every test is announced, and not every observation is obvious, but integrity is always being measured, even when no one says a word.

So as you move along your journey, be mindful. Be watchful above all things for the darts, arrows, and traps that may come your way. Stay ready and stand firm. (Read Epistle to the Ephesians 6:11–13, KJV.) These verses remind us: *"Put on the whole armour of God, that ye may be able to stand against the wiles of the devil... Wherefore take unto you the whole armour of God, that ye may be able to withstand in the evil day, and having done all, to stand."*

After that... go for it, man. Go for it. And take this with you along your journey. Move forward with confidence, but also with discernment.

Walk with strength, but also with humility. And remember that every step you take is shaping not only your future, but also the example you leave behind for those who are watching and learning from your life.

Fear Not Responsibility

Full speed ahead like a high speed train.
Fear not responsibility,
think only of the gain.
Love, respect, and most of all no debt.
Learn what you can, especially responsibility.
The more responsibility the
harder you'll work.
And the more you'll appreciate
what you have.
So, fear not responsibility.

Chapter 4

Don't Be a Bitter Man; Be a Better Man

Chapter 4
Don't be a Bitter Man; Be a Better Man

Think about this: In order for her to act a certain way, you have to treat her a certain way. Ask yourself: How do I want her to act? What must I do to get the response I want? Do I want happiness, surprise, or something else?

At this point, the ball is in your court, so think it through carefully. Once you put that energy out there, there's no taking it back. If you hurt her feelings, you can't undo that either. So, be clear and intentional. Remember, that could be you on the receiving end, and how would you want to be treated?

Now, let's be real. How do you expect to attract a woman when you don't have yourself together? The truth is, they choose us; we don't choose them. (You didn't know that, did you?) She has to see something in you that she genuinely likes, something that appeals to her.

Let me break it down for you:

- Your money, your car
- Your clothes, your scent
- Your appearance, the way you smile at her
- Your home, your lifestyle

Some of these things may reflect who you truly are, and some may not. Or, maybe it's that one unique thing you do, something she really likes, but you're unaware of it until she lets you in on her little secret about you. Then, and only then, do you become the icing on the cake. But until then, you're not doing much of anything. So I'll say it again, my brother: Get it together. And if I were you, I'd do it fast.

Let me leave you with one of my favorite quotes: "Don't be a bitter man; be a better man." Now, let me ask you something else. Do you have a child or children? If so, then you likely have one or more of the following in your life, a wife, a girlfriend, a fiancée, or a child's mother, whatever your situation may be.

And with that often comes someone we all recognize: Ms. Drama. We don't like her, because she tends to insert herself into everything. She isn't happy, and she doesn't want anyone else to be happy either. As the saying goes, "Misery loves company." So whatever you do, make it your business to communicate with whoever you need to in order to keep the peace, for the sake of you and your children. Everyone communicates differently, so be mindful of that.

Talk to your significant other about the situation. Give her a heads-up, so she's not caught off guard when conflict arises. That way, you can handle things quickly and appropriately, without unnecessary disruption to your family. Be clear. Be honest. Be precise. Because at the end of the day, you don't want anything to negatively affect your relationship with your children.

CHAPTER 5

ACT RIGHT

CHAPTER 5
ACT RIGHT

This is where you need to sit down like adults and have an honest conversation about the situation at hand. Make it clear that respect is not optional; it's necessary. "If you love me, then there's a certain level of respect that I need." Have this conversation on a personal level, one-on-one, so no one feels like they're being put on display or that you're trying to grandstand in front of others. Keep it real, keep it private, and keep it respectful. This kind of dialogue requires maturity, emotional control, and the willingness to listen just as much as you speak. It is not about winning an argument; it is about preserving dignity and establishing boundaries that protect the relationship.

Once you've had that adult conversation, accept the outcome for what it is. Not every discussion ends perfectly, but clarity is still progress. After that, it's time to speak to your child or children, depending on their age. Because when the adults are around the kids, there's a standard of behavior that has to be upheld. Acting out, arguing, or being disrespectful in front of them, who does that really affect? Your children. Children are more perceptive than many adults realize; they absorb tone, tension, and energy even when no words are spoken.

The reality is simple: I might not like you, and you might not like me. But in front of our children, we get along. That's the agreement. Also, the women involved might not like each other either. But around the children, they find a way to coexist, if not fully get along, then at least maintain peace. Because the goal here is bigger than personal feelings. The goal is to protect the children. And also, to protect your image in their eyes. Because whether you realize it or not, someone is always watching, even when you don't see them. Every interaction becomes a memory they will carry into adulthood, shaping how they view relationships, conflict, and resolution.

Here's something to think about: I can put all of my children's mothers in one room together, and they would get along. Why? Out of respect for me. Because, for the most part, I've carried myself as a good man. Now ask yourself, how many of you can say that? With a clean heart and a clear conscience? That didn't happen by accident. It reflects how I was raised, how I was guided, and how I chose to respond to life's challenges. Respect is not demanded; it is demonstrated over time.

To my mom, my stepdad, and my dad, thank you. Mom, you showed me how not to treat a woman. I learned early that you never put your hands on a woman in a violent way. That lesson stuck with me and became a moral boundary I would not cross. Dad, you showed me how to be a man, a family man, a provider, and a gentleman. Those lessons shaped my understanding of responsibility, leadership, and presence.

Both my stepdad and my biological father taught me the value of hard work. That it's okay to get your hands dirty while grinding to take care of your family. Each of them, in their own way and on their own time, gave me the same message: "You always treat them good. That way, no matter how they feel about you, they'll never forget you." That principle became more than instruction. It became a way of life, a standard for how I choose to carry myself in every relationship and responsibility.

But that raises a real question: How much can one man take? Not just physically or emotionally, but relationally, mentally, and spiritually. How much pressure, misunderstanding, and expectation can a man carry while still striving to remain balanced, respectful, and true to who he is?

Chapter 6

The Post and The Most

Chapter 6
The Post and The Most

On the brink of destruction, another marriage hangs in the balance. Between the constant arguing and ongoing conflict, the threats of leaving, and talk of divorce, everything feels like it's unraveling. Both sides are caught in a cycle of being right - and wrong - at the same time. What begins as disagreement slowly becomes distance, and what starts as conversation turns into confrontation. Over time, emotional fatigue sets in, and even the smallest issues begin to feel heavier than they really are.

So what is a real man supposed to do? Keep settling for the short end of the stick just to maintain a little peace? Maybe at first. But eventually, that wears thin. At some point, there has to be real balance, give and take on both sides. And right now, that means she may need to give a little more. Not in submission, but in understanding. In space. In respect. Because at this stage, as a man, you may feel like you've already given everything and then some. This is where emotional exhaustion meets expectation, and where many men begin to feel unseen or unheard in the very place they are expected to find peace.

Let's be honest about it. You've been:

- The leaning post
- The whipping post
- The host without the most
- The one cussed out the most
- The one threatened the most
- The one who stayed quiet the most
- The one who put up with the most
- And the one belittled the most

And too often, that becomes the silent reality for many men. These experiences are rarely discussed openly, yet they accumulate over time. Then, add fatherhood into the mix and the weight only increases. The responsibilities, the expectations, the pressure to hold everything together. And still, you're expected to endure without breaking. Then, people wonder why you start looking for a way out. What is often misunderstood is that the desire to leave is not always about lack of love. It is sometimes about depletion, about a man reaching the edge of what he believes he can emotionally carry.

But here's the turning point: Instead of only looking for an exit, start working on yourself. Not as a form of escape from responsibility, but as a path toward restoration, clarity, and strength. Because when a man begins to invest in his own emotional, mental, and spiritual development, he stops merely reacting to life and starts actively shaping it.

Because this part right here is for the men. This concerns you, my brother. Statistics show that 1 in 4 men have experienced some form of physical violence by an intimate partner. This can include slapping, shoving, or pushing, behaviors that, in many cases, fall in the category of domestic violence. About 1 in 25 men have been injured by an intimate partner. And 1 in 10 men in the United States have experienced rape, physical violence, and/or stalking. The numbers may shift over time, but the reality doesn't change: this is happening, and it's often overlooked. These are not just statistics; they represent real men, real homes, and real silent struggles that are frequently hidden behind pride, fear, or misunderstanding.

So ask yourself honestly: What category do you fall into? What side of the spectrum are you on - victim or abuser? There's no shame in facing the truth. But there is danger in avoiding it. Self-awareness is not weakness; it is the beginning of change. It is the moment a man chooses honesty over denial, and growth over stagnation.

Help is out there. There are programs, resources, and organizations in every city and state ready to support you, whether you need protection, guidance, or accountability. You don't have to carry it all alone. Reaching out is not a sign of failure. It is a step toward healing, stability, and rebuilding a stronger foundation for yourself and those connected to your life.

Chapter 7

Manhood 101

CHAPTER 7
MANHOOD 101

We're all human; therefore, we make mistakes. The hope is that we learn from them and bounce back, stronger each time. Every now and then, life is going to hit you, and you've got to take it on the chin. That's part of manhood. It is not the absence of failure that defines a man, but his response to it. A man is measured not only by how he stands in victory, but also by how he rises after defeat, disappointment, and delay. Every setback carries within it a lesson, and every lesson carries within it the possibility of growth, if you are willing to see it.

Sometimes, what comes your way won't sit right with you. It challenges the inner man, the part of you that thinks, questions, and feels. Meanwhile, the outer man wants to react, to act, to handle things in ways he already knows. But is that always the best move? Is it right, or is it wrong? Now you're thinking, and that's where wisdom begins. That tension between emotion and response is where maturity is formed.

Learning not to be controlled by impulse is one of the first steps toward real stability in life.

Remember, there's a cause and effect in every situation. Every action carries a consequence. Before you move, take a moment to think about the possible outcomes. That pause, that awareness, that's Manhood 101. That pause is not weakness; it is strength under control. It is the ability to govern yourself before the situation governs you.

Manhood 102

You have to live with your results. There are no do-overs, no rewinds. The inner man thinks deeply; the outer man moves quickly. Somewhere between the two is where you find balance. Get in where you fit in - no judgment here. This is just a real conversation. Life does not always offer second chances in the way we wish it would, which is why decisions must be weighed carefully before they become consequences that must be carried.

I'm not here to make you comfortable. I'm here to strike a chord, maybe even hit a nerve, because sometimes that's what it takes to wake up. Open your eyes. Get up from doing nothing and start producing something - something real, something legal, something that builds an income and a future. Comfort can be dangerous when it keeps a man stagnant. Growth often begins where comfort ends.

Understand this: The gap between where you are and where you want to be often comes down to education and money, both of which create opportunity. And yes, what you know matters, but who you know can open doors knowledge alone cannot. Connections matter. Don't forget that. However, connections without preparation are wasted opportunities. You must be ready when doors open, not just hopeful that they will.

You say you're hard? Let me tell you what hard really is. Hard is waking up at 5 a.m., five to seven days a week. Showing up at all kinds of hours, even when you don't feel like it. Doing what needs to be done anyway. That's hard. Being "hard" is one thing. Doing what's hard is something else entirely, especially when your life depends on it. Discipline is what separates intention from impact. Many speak strength, but fewer live it in consistency.

So ask yourself: how much does your life depend on your discipline, your choices, your actions? Let that sink in. I talk to my brothers, men of all colors, all walks of life. We share a language that doesn't always need words. Even if it's just for a few minutes, we come away with something, some understanding, some truth. Like this one: You can't truly love anyone else until you learn to love yourself first. That truth is not just emotional. It is foundational. Because the way you treat yourself will eventually shape the way you treat everyone connected to you.

About the Author

Warren Watkins, Jr. is a native of Baltimore, Maryland, who now lives in the mountains of Pennsylvania. He's an actor, author, and award winning poet, who played in the HBO series *The Wire* and *Ladder 49*. He also played in Music in my Soul, a stage play written by Ramona Jones-Maddox.

In 1999 and 2000, he self-published the following books:
*1999 - Love Is Like Poetry
*2000 - A Man And HIs Stories

His poetry has been seen in anthologies, such as:
*On The Wings of Pegasus (Famous Poets Society)
*By The Light of The Moon (National Library of Poetry)

He has won the following awards:
1999 -Editor's Choice Award
2001 - 2002-Poet of the Year
2002 - Shakespeare Trophy of Excellence

In 2010, he moved to California, and in 2012, he released *Introducing The Secret Pen* published by CLF Publishing Collaborative, LLC.

Now in 2026, he's back with this intriguing text *Manhood Mangood* (A Healing Conversation).

www.ingramcontent.com/pod-product-compliance
Lightning Source LLC
LaVergne TN
LVHW052338100826
845147LV00020B/1111

* 9 7 9 8 9 9 2 5 7 8 4 5 4 *